A Collection Of Coats Of Arms Borne By The Nobility And Gentry Of The County Of Glocester

Engraver Ames

Alpha Editions

This Edition Published in 2021

ISBN: 9789354442698

Design and Setting By
Alpha Editions
www.alphaedis.com
Email – info@alphaedis.com

As per information held with us this book is in Public Domain.
This book is a reproduction of an important historical work. Alpha Editions
uses the best technology to reproduce historical work in the same manner
it was first published to preserve its original nature. Any marks or number
seen are left intentionally to preserve its true form.

 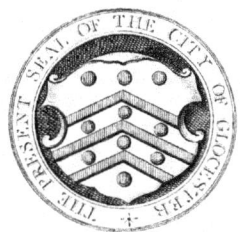

INTRODUCTION.

THE design of this publication is an accurate display of Coats of Arms, borne by the Nobility and Gentry of the county of *Glocester*.— These are arranged in three divisions; in the first, those Arms that are prefixed to Sir *Robert Atkins*'s History, of the edition of 1712, which included the most respectable families of that age. From what documents these were collected, we are not informed, for in the courfe of that work no Arms are recorded as the decoration of houfes, windows, or fepulchral monuments.

As tranfmitted, they are faithfully inferted; not, we truft, without propriety, as an interefting part of a County Hiftory, which owes not its prefent value folely to its fcarcenefs, but as being the production of a man eminently converfant in the local hiftory of his country, and of that province in particular, where his poffeffions and influence were fo extenfive.

In point of accuracy, he was certainly deficient, fo far as it refpected the ftate of parochial affairs in his own time; but in his accounts of the earlier gradations of property, as his fources of intelligence were the grand records of the nation, he was comprehenfive and exact. To extenuate the firft charge of *negligence*, we muft confider, that his eminent ftation precluded the labour of perfonal inveftigation, and actual furvey. Much was left to cafual information; and where report is adopted without examination, there muft neceffarily be error.—It may not be improper to obferve, that it is much more eafy to correct his errors, than improve his plan by a total alteration; and the more ready way to doubt, than to invalidate his authorities.

In the year 1779, Mr. *Rudder*, of *Cirencester*, published, according to proposals, a " New History of *Glocestershire*," as an improvement on Sir *Robert*'s plan, as including Arms, monumental Inscriptions, Genealogies, and Memoirs, deduced to that period, and not to be found in the former work. How far he has excelled the first History, it is not necessary to enquire.—With his Heraldry all our business rests. None of the Arms which he has registered are engraven, which suggested the idea of exhibiting them emblazoned, as alphabetically arranged in his index. This constitutes the second part.

The third division comprises such Arms as are not in either history of the county, and such only who have generoufly encouraged this attempt. The Editor hopes that none will be difpleafed at the omiffion of Coats of Arms not duly certified, as he cannot prefume to interfere with the juft and anciently eftablifhed rights of the *College of Arms*.

A full difquifition of the fubject of Heraldry will not be expected. That it was introduced during the Crufades, as furnifhing badges of diftinction to Knights and Efquires, is a matter of general notoriety. To form fome conclufion in what proportion thefe honors were diftributed, an account is fubjoined (for the gratification of the curious) of the names of thofe Knights of this county, who ferved in the army of King *Henry* III. about a century after the more general introduction of Heraldry into this kingdom. This lift, in the *French* of that age, is copied verbatim from a manufcript authenticated and publifhed in the *Antiquarian Repertory*.

Les Noms de Chivaliers en le Champ du Roy Henri III.

A. D. 1220.

GLOCESTERSCIRE.

1. SIR OLIVER DE SEINT AMAUND,

Port Or, frette fable et la chefe fable et iij. marles argente.

2. Sir WYLLIAM BEAUCHAMP,

Goulis, et une fefe enter 6 marles or, et bourdure endentè argente.

3. Sir JOHAN DE WICHAM,

Sable et une fefe enter 6 marles argente.

4. Sir ROBERT LE FITZ PAYNE,

Goulis, iij. lions paffans argente et une bende gobonnè or et azure.

5. Sir GILBERT PAUNCEVOD,

Goulis, iij. lioncels argente.

6. Sir HAMOND L'ESTRANGE,

Goulis, ij. lions paffans argente et une bend or.

7. Sir JOHN L'ESTRANGE,

Goulis les marles or, et ij. lions paffans argente.

8. Sir JOHN L'ESTRANGE,

Goulis, ij. lions paffans argente, et la bordure endentè or, et une bend azure.

9. Sir ROBERT DE FELTON,

Goulis, ij. lions paffans armyn.

10. Sir JOHN DE FELTON,

Mefmes les armys coronès de or.

11. Sir WILLIAM FELTON,

Goulis, et ij. lions paffans argente, et une bend gobonnè or et azure.

12. Sir GYLBERT DE KNOUVYLE,

Argente et iij. moles goulis.

13. Sir JOHN DE KNOUVYLE,

Mesmes les armys, et une labell azure.

14. Sir EDMUND BASSET,

Armyn, et la chefe goulis endentè, et iij. escallops or.

15. Sir JOHN BASSET,

Or, la chefe goulis endentè, a iij. moles de or.

16. Sir NICHOLAS DE VELERES,

Argente une croise goulis, et cinque escallops or.

17. Sir NICHOLAS DE SEMMOR,

Argente et ij. chevrons goulis, et une labell vert.

18. Sir WALTER DE GLOUCESTER,

Argente et iij. lioncels goulis, et la bordure en-dentè azure.

19. Sir WARYN MARTYN,

Argente ij. barris goulis befantés.

20. Sir GILBERT TALBOT,

Goulis, une lion rampand or, et la bordure en-dentè or.

21. Sir SIMON GYFFORDE,

Goulis, et iij. lions paffans argente, et une labell fable.

22. Sir PERS DE BROUSE,

Or, croiselè sable, et une lion rampand sable, la cowe forché, renowé.

23. Sir RICHARD DE ANTESHEYE,

Party or et argente undy goulis.

24. Sir RICHARD DE ASTON,

Goulis, et une lion rampand or, et une bend vert.

25. Sir WILLIAM DE WANTON,

Argente, une chevron sable, et iij. egles or.

26. Sir THOMAS DE BARKELEY,

Goulis, et les rosettes argente, et une chevron argente.

27. Sir JOHN DE BERKELEY,

Goulis, iij. crois patés de or, et une chevron argente.

28. Sir RICHARD DE STAKEPOLE,

Argente, une lion rampand goulis, et la coler or.

29. Sir WALTER BASKERVILE,

Argente, et iij. roundelles azure, et une chevron goulis, croiselé or.

30. Sir ROGER LE ROUS,

Party or et azure, et iij. lioncells goulis.

31. Sir JOHN LE ROUS,

Party azure et goulis, et iij. lioncells armynes.

32. Sir WILLIAM DE HOTOT,

De azure a iij. creſſans argente une chevron de or.

33. Sir JOHN DE HOTOT,

Les meſmes armys, et la chevron gemelé.

34. Sir WILLIAM MAUNSELL,

Goulis, une feſe argente et une labell argente.

35. S. ABLEHALE,

Or, une feſe goulis.

36. Sir EDMUND DE WELINGTON,

Goulis, une fautour veer, en la chefe une molet or.

37. Sir WALTER BLUET,

Or, une chevron enter iij. egles vert.

38. Sir WILLIAM DE LONGE,

Goulis, et une fautour engralé or.

39. Sir THOMAS CIRCESTRE,

Argente, une chevron azure, et une labell goulis.

40. Sir WALTER HUKEFORD,

Or, une egle sable, et une coler argente.

41. Sir HENRY DE WELLEMSCOT,

Argente, et ij. barris azure, et une lion rampand goulis, coroné or.

42. Sir HEWE DE AUDLEY,

Goulis, fretté or, et une labell azure.

43. Sir JAMES DE AUDLEY,

Mesmes les armys, en la labell les lioncells or.

44. Sir JOHAN DE HASTINGES,

Or, une manche goulis, et la bordure de valence.

45. Sir JOHN DE RATTENDEN,

Azure, et les marles argente.

46. Sir WALTER DE OPTONE,

Goulis, croisfelé or, et une lion rampand or.

47. Sir JOHN DE WYNSINGTON,

Sable et iij. teſtes de ſinglere argente.

48. Sir PAYNE TORBERVYLE,

Checker or et goulis, et une feſe armyn.

49. Sir JOHN NORREYS,

Sable, beletté argente, et une crois argente la chefe florrettè.

50. Sir LEYSONE DE ANENE,

Goulis, iij. chevronells argente.

51. Sir WYLLIAM DE BASKERVLES,

Azure, une chevron enter iij. creſſans or.

52. Sir JOHN DE CARRU,

Or, iij. lioncells paſſans et une labell goulis.

53. Sir NICHOLAS DE CLARE,

Or, iij. chevronells goulis, et la bordure endenté ſable.

54. Sir GILBERT DE ST. AUWYN,

Goulis, iij. chevrons or.

55. Sir WILLIAM DE FLEMINGES,

De goulis fretté et de argente, a une feſe de azure.

In the *Bodlean* Library, MSS. *Dodfworth*, is a List of the same kind, certified in the second of *Edward* II. 1309, in which many of these names occur, and the whole number is encreased to eighty.

Though it might now be difficult to describe what property these individually held in this county, yet we may well conclude, that some good reason may be alledged why they should be attributed to *Glocesterſhire*, in an account of their fellow Knights of every province in the nation. But these are matters of antiquarian research, rather than immediately connected with our present subject *.

---

* Of the grants of the celebrated *Camden*, which, during his Office of *Clarencieux*, amounted to 159, eight only are to families of this

A test of the antiquity of a Coat of Arms is in general its simplicity, a single ordinary, or two at most, constituting the most noble.

Forma quid hæc simplex? simplex fuit ipsa vetustas.
Simplicitas formæ stemmata prisca notat.
HIERON. HENNINGS, GENEALOG.

Crosses of all distinctions became a general bearing in the time of the crusades, and were borne in proportion to the number of exploits performed

---

county, as we find them recorded in *Morgan's Heraldry*, page 107.

1. Sir *Leonard Halliday*, Knt. of *Rodborough*, Lord Mayor of *London*. 1605.
2. ——— *Stephens*, of *Eastington*. 1605.
3. *Thomas Estcourte*, of *Shipton Moigne*. 1606.
4. *Daniel Fowler*, of *Stonehouse*. 1606.
5. *Richard Wood*, of *Brockrup*.
6. ——— *Bowser*, of *Stone*.
7. ——— *Codrington*, of *Codrington*.
8. ——— *Smith*, of *Campden*.

in thofe wars by the bearers of them. We are told by *Guillim*, that the *Fleur de Lis* was worn as an enfign by thofe who had done military fervices in either invafion of *France* by the *Englifh*.—The *Garb* or *Sheaf* is a charge peculiar to the Nobility and Gentry of *Chefhire*, as being the cognizance of *Gilbert le Grofvenour*, nephew of *Hugh Lupus*, eftablifhed as the firft Count Palatine by *William the Conqueror*, and is ufually borne by families connected with that county.

Bezants were firft borne by the foldiers of the Holy Wars, being the current coin of *Byzantium* (the modern *Conftantinople*) with which the ftipends of the army were difcharged.

The *Mullet* is properly the rowel of a spur, (from the *French Molette*), and not a star of five points. The *Estoile* is *usually* radiated. Mullets were borne by those of knightly houses, particularly when of gold.

Martlets, as birds of passage, were used by foreigners of all nations settled here; but particularly by the descendants of those who attended the victorious *William*.

Annulets were granted in coat armour to those who were in confidence, or entrusted with especial commissions by the King: the Annulet or Ring being the gage of the royal favour and protection.

Efcallops were the peculiar badge of thofe who had performed religious pilgrimages to the Holy Sepulchre on *Mount Calvary*. The Pilgrims or Palmers were diftinguifhed from other *Religious* by their Cockle or Efcallop worn in the hat, and their *Potent*, an ancient word fignifying a Crutch, in which fenfe we read it in *Chaucer*,

> " So eld that fhee ne went
> " Afoote, but it were by *Potent*."

From hence a kind of faƈtitious Fur was invented, refembling the Heads of Crutches oppofed to each other, called *Potent Counter-Potent*.

Crefcents are faid by fome writers to allude to viƈtories over the *Turks ;* and defcribed by others as being adopted by the second houses of great families, or by men who have become eminent from mean origin.

Several reasons are given why the arms of Females should be displayed on a *Lozenge* or *Fufil**.—The Lozenge is now more generally supposed to have been a Cushion of that shape, and the Fusil is evidently the Spindle used in spinning, both demonstrative of the sedentary employments of women.

Of the more common ordinaries, the derivation is more easily ascertained. The *Bend* was a Sash

---

* *Morgan*, in his *Treatise on Heraldry*, supposes the Lozenge to have been a Jewel or Ornament of that shape worn by Ladies in their head-dresses, and usually decorated with some heraldic distinction.

worn across the shoulders, from the *Italian*, *La Benda*. The *Feſſe* a Girdle or Belt. The *Chevron* was two Pales placed in that form to mark out the ground in tournaments. The *Saltier* was an engine uſed in ſcaling walls.—Moſt of theſe have their diminutives, when borne in greater number in the ſame eſcutcheon.

The diſhonorable ordinaries, or abatements of honour, were a *Delph*, a *Point Dexter*, a *Point in Point*, a *Point Champion*, a *Point Plain*, a *Gore Siniſter*, and *two Guſſets* *. The laws of chivalry, which had ever the redreſs of injuries, and the eſtabliſhment of juſt rights, as their invariable object, ap-

---

* *Blome's Eſſay on Heraldry*, Edit. 1685.

pointed these abatements, as a punishment of delinquency against the military code, or the common good of society.—But abatements were usually confined to military offences, such as killing prisoners during capitulation, revoking a challenge, or flying colours; and even for slighter faults, as intemperate boasting, or criminal neglect of discipline. In cases of treason, *the Escutcheon* was *totally reversed.* When the peace of private families was invaded by adultery or rape, the delinquent was forced to bear the *Inescutcheon reversed,* or *the Gussets,* as a badge of his infamy.—In every instance of armorial degradation, *the Metals,* being in themselves specifically noble, could not be borne as emblazoning the disgraceful charges, which were required to be either *Sanguine* or *Tenne*, colours commonly ufed to fignify difhonor. It would be repugnant to thofe principles of juftice, which were the characteriftic of chivalry, to fuppofe that this *Stigma* was ever tranfmitted to pofterity. The punifhment was merely perfonal, and proportioned in point of duration to the nature of the offence. On which account *we* hardly know that fuch ordinaries were ever ufed; indeed, in the prefent ftate of a fcience fo obfolete, they muft univerfally fail of their intended effect.

From the enthufiaftic love of equity and honor, that marked the darker ages, the fpirit of chivalry arofe. Its general influence and romantic motives are attributed by *the moderns* more to the force of the imagination, than the dictates of sound judgement; and as produced rather by general barbarism, than partial refinements.

Upon these institutes, the science of Heraldry was formed, while by its connection with the graphic art, it could add external ornament to the *Meritorious*, by delineations of rude invention, and shapeless splendour.— These are the only remains of antiquity, from which the hand of modern improvement has abstained. And who would wish to exchange for the more polished inventions of later times, *Devices*, which have ever been regarded with a kind of religious veneration?

We might enlarge this digreſſion, but are unwilling to obtrude on thoſe that know, or to weary the patience of thoſe who are ignorant of this particular ſcience.

In the later centuries, Arms* were more general, becauſe moſt men of property, without military acquirements, pretended to them. In the year 1484, King *Richard* the Third eſtabliſhed the *College of Arms*, on its preſent foundation, inveſting them with full powers of ſummoning thoſe that

---

* The *Welſh* Families, amongſt other pretenſions to antiquity, have collectively but few Coats of Arms, the ſame being borne by many different names. *Ellis, Bodville* and *Bodurda, Jenkins, Hughes, Griffidth, Williams,* and *Richards,* bear *Sable a chevron between three fleurs de lis argente,* as being derived from *Colwyn,* one of the Princes of the Fifteen Tribes of *Gwynedd,* or *North Wales.* CAMDEN.

assumed the arms of others, to appear in the Earl Marshal's Court, and of granting Escutcheons to families of newly acquired consequence. This privilege multiplied the figures of course, and varied the differences. Forms of every description in the infancy of the graphic art, without any exact resemblance, if we may judge from the specimens now remaining, were universally introduced.

The creation was exhausted in the representation of the different parts of it, and to gothic fancy alone we owe the introduction of Gryphons, Mermaids, Wyverns, and Harpies. Every invention of art, whether military or mechanic, has been at one time or other a badge of heraldic honor. When the Arms referred abfolutely to furnames, they were called by the *French, Les Armes parlantes,—Canting or punning Arms,*—and thefe, though fome ancient precedents exift, were not common 'till the commencement of the feventeenth century, when they prevailed under the aufpices of King *James*. This circumftance proves moft of them to be of modern date.

" The hereditary ufe of Arms was not eftablifhed till the reign of *Henry* III. The laft Earls of *Chefter*, the *Quinceys*, Earls of *Winchefter*, and the *Lacies*, Earls of *Lincoln*, varied ftill the father from the fon."—The *Veres* and *Berkeleys* altered their paternal Coats, when " they had taken up the Crofs," the phrase of that day for engaging in the Holy Wars. Gentlemen at that time usually bore the Arms (or at least the principal ordinary of them) of those Noblemen or Knights from whom they held lands in fee, or under whose banner they fought. We find in *Camden* (*Remains*, p. 214) that *Hubertus de Burgo*, Earl of *Kent*, who bore for his Arms, " Gules seven lozenges vairè," granted lands at *Elmore*, in this county, to *Anselmus de Guise*, 2d of *Edward* I. 1274; whereupon the said *Anselmus* bare the same Coat, with a canton or, charged with a mullet pierced sable, for difference*.

---

* Arms were in some instances bequeathed by will from a Knight to his Esquire. They were likewise alienated by voluntary cession during

In the present age, when the great influx of wealth by commerce hath elevated many of mean origine into the rank of Gentry, a Coat of Arms is usually granted or assumed to support the pretension. In some instances the bearings, which are attached to particular names, are assumed by

---

life, as well as testamentary bequest. The form of the second mode is recorded as being ratified by the following instrument :—

Noverint universi per præsentes me Johannam *nuper uxorem* Gulielmi Lee, *de* Knightly *Dominam & rectam hæredem de* Knightly *dedisse concessisse hâc præsenti cartâ meâ confirmâsse* Ricardo Pesthale, *filio* Humfredi Pesthale, *scutum armorum meorum habend. & tenend. ac portand. & utend. ubicunque voluerit sibi & hæredibus suis in perpetuum. Ita quod nec ego, nec aliquis alius in nomine meo aliquid jus vel clamium in prædicto scuto habere potuerimus sed per præsentes sumus exclusi in perpetuum. In cujus, rei testimonium, sigillum meum opposui. Dat. anno regni* Hen. IV. 14º. 1412.

A distinction was then made between a *Gentleman of Blood* and a *Gentleman of Coat Armour*, who was the first of family who bore Arms; from whom the third only in lineal descent was considered and enrolled as a *Gentleman of Blood*. CAMDEN UT SUPRA.

[33]

all of the fame, when they are not otherwife provided. It is common to obferve, that thofe of real family pretenfions infift on them with arrogance; while the low born man of wealth returns the contempt, with juft reflections on the inefficacy of confequence, that has ceafed for ages.

With regard to genealogical deductions and rights of quartering, we muft confine ourfelves to thofe Arms only that occur in Mr. *Rudder*'s Hiftory, on fepulchral monuments.

To a candid public, this little compilation is humbly fubmitted, with hopes that it may be found to amufe, where it cannot inform.

K

To thofe, who have encouraged this work by a liberal fubfcription, the Editor returns his grateful acknowledgments, trufting, that in their reception of it, they will not withold an indulgence, which he has deferved only by his labour to obtain.

ARMS BORNE QUARTERLY

PER PALE,

AND ON AN

ESCUTCHEON OF PRETENCE;

COLLECTED FROM

RUDDER's HISTORY of GLOCESTERSHIRE.

BORNE QUARTERLY.

A.

Abercherder, by *Innys*

Argent, a lion rampant gules, by *Thynne*

Argent, a faltier azure, by *Slaughter*

Azure, a crofs crofslet fitchè and *Keck*, by *Tracy*

B.

Baillie, by *Hamilton*

Baker, by *Dowell*

Browning, Efcutcheon of Pretence

Bell, Clutterbuck, and *Clifford,* by *Winchcombe*
1. *Bloet.* 2. *Brotherton.* 3. *Mowbray.* 4. *Breaus.* 5. *Seagrave.* 6. *Chancombes.* 7. *Longefpey.* 8. *Albency.* 9. *Fitz-Allen.* 10. *Blundevyle.* 11. *Warren.* 12. *Plantagenet.* 13. *Marshall.* 14. *Strongbow.* 15. *Murchard.* 16. *Mead.* 17. *Read.* and 18. *Stanhope,* by Earl *Berkeley*

Bourchier, by *Rich*

Bottetort, by *Berkeley,*—Baronefs *Bottetort*

Boevey, by *Crawley*

C.

Cliffe, by *Batefon*

Clifford, by *Clutterbuck*

Clopton and *Burton,* by *Lingen*

Cocks, by *Stanford*
1. *Corbet.* 2. *Ruffel.* 3. *Pennington.* 4. *Gorges.* 5. *Danvers.* 6. two bars on a chief, 3 flag's heads

[37]

cabofhed. 7. *Still*, by *Dennis Coffins* and *Savile*, by *Marriffal*.

D.

1. *Dobyns*. 2. *Berkeley*. and 3. Gules, a ftag's head cabofhed or, by *Yate*

E.

Edwards, by *Freeman*

F.

Field, by *Phelps*

G.

1. Gules, a chief counter componé or et azure over all a bend argent.
2. Azure, a lion rampant between 8 crofs crofslets fitchè argent.
3. Gules on a chief argent 3 martlets fable.
4. *De Barry*. 5. *Pembridge*. 6. *Newman*. 7. Argent, a bend void. gules in chief a rofe, by *De la Bere*.
1. Gules, a feffe between

[38]

six billets or. 2. Sable, a fesse between 3 martlets argent, by *Guise*.

H.

1. Gules, a lion rampant or, debruised of a bend ermine. 2. Or, a bend sable between 6 pellets, by *Hill*.

Hall, by *Brown*
Hale, by *Blagden*
Heydon, by *Peachy*
Huddlestone, by *De la Bere*

J.

Jermye, *Roe*, and *Tempest*, by *Berkeley*

L.

Lovell, by *Innys*
Lucy by *Keyt*
1. *Lygon*. 2. *Bracy*. 3. *Madresfield*. 4. *Harefleet*. 5. *Decors*. 6. *Giffard*. 7. *Beauchamp*. 8. *Abtot*. 9. *Uffleet*. 10. *Furnival*. 11. *Laftoft*. 12. *Verdon*. 13. *Greville*. 14. *Arie*. and 15. *Southie*, by *Dormer*

1. *Menfeir.* 2. *Bates.* 3. *Swan*, and *Shilling*, by *Graves*

M.

Mowbray, Warren, and *Brotherton*, by Earl of *Effingham*

P.

1. *Pigot.* 2. Gules 3 lioncels in pale argent. 3. *Lucy.* 4. Party per feffe et per pale indented argent and fable 4 bu- gle horns counterchanged, by *Finch*

1. *Pool.* 2. *Solers*, and on a bend 4 roundlets, by *Whittington*

Pury, by *Whittington*

Pytts, by *Batefon*

S.

Sable, a feffe between 3 falcon's heads erafed or, by *Eftcourt*

Saunders, by *Guife*

Smyth, by *Ball*

Snell, by *Guife*

Stowel, Olepenne, Baſſet, Throgmorton, Huſſey, Bridgeman, Jones, Lowe, Clayton, Turner, Knollys, and Singe, alias Millington, by Daunt

Stephens, by De la Bere

T.

Tankerville by Chamberlayne

Tregoz, Wantham, Baldeſmere, Grandiſon Herte, Gralle, Elton, and Giſſard, by Norwood

Treville by Burthogge

W.

Wyvely, by Lippincott

V.

Villiers, Apſley, and Petre, by Earl Bathurſt

IMPALED;

OR, ON AN

ESCUTCHEON OF PRETENCE.

A.

Adye, by *Ainge*

Adey, by *Blagden*

Argent, a bend vert between a mullet in chief, and an annulet in base gules, by *Keyte*

Argent, on a chevron, between 3 lozenges sable 3 stag's heads caboshed or, by *Rich*

Azure, a bend between 3 leopard's faces or, by *Sandford*

Arnold, by *Cole*

Arnold, by *Porter*

Audley, and *Strange*, by *Nicholas*

Aylworth, by *Elyott*

B.

Bateſon, by *Sambach*
Baugh, by *Hancock*
Baynham, by *Clutterbuck*
Baynton, and *King*, by *Dutton*
Bedford, by *Colborne*
Bernard, by *Bedford*
Blagden, by *Adey*
Blagden, by *Oſborne*
Blathwayte, by *Southwell*
Blycke, by *Clare*
Bray, by *Stephens*
Brereton, by *Bourchier*
Bridgeman, by *Burgoyne*
Bridges, by *Neaſt*
Brown, by *Blomer*
Bruce, by *Bathurſt*, Eſcutcheon of Pretence
Bull by *Stephens*
Burthogge, by *Stephens*
Byrd, by *Brawne*

C.

Calvert, by *Paſton*
Capel, by *Somerſet*
Carteret, by *Atkins*
Chapman, by *Driver*
Chapman, by *Codrington*
Clarke, by *Colcheſter*

Checquy, on a chief a rofe, by *Uvedade*

Codrington, by *Horler*

Cocks, by *Percye*

Cole, by *Driver*

Cooke, by *Guife*, Efcutcheon of Pretence

Colchefter, by *Roberts*

Coffins, by *Innys*

Courtenay, by *Pafton*, Efcutcheon of Pretence

Coventry, by *Thynne*

Creed, by *Campbell*, Efcutcheon of Pretence

Crewe, by *Adey*

Cartwright, by *Partridge*

Chichefter, by *Pafton*

D.

De la Bere, by *Baghott*, Efcutcheon of Pretence

Dowdefwell, by *Knight*

Dodwell, by *Tracy*, Efcutcheon of Pretence

Dunch, by *Wade*

Draper, by *Webb*

E.

Elliot, by *Cocks*

Engeham, by *Nourfe*

Escourt, by *Hodges*

Eyer, by *Newton*

F.

Fane, by *Henley*

Fox, by *Bigland*

Fuller, by *Dodwell*

Fuſt by *Warner*

G.

Georges, by *Powell*

Gilbert, by *Rich*

Gibbes, by *Harrington*

Godfrey, by *Bourne*

Greville, by *Tame*

Greville, by *Berkeley*

Gregory, by *Arundell*

Gules 3 creſcents or. by *Adey*

Gules a dexter arm vambraced or. by *Fream*

Gyde, by *Clutterbuck*

Gyde, by *Adey*

Gyde, by *Mills*

H.

Hall, by *Wakeman*

Hickes, by *Banniſter*

Hickes, by *Purnell*

Hill, by *Field*

Hill, by *Pinfold*

Harmer, by *Jefferies*

Harrington, by *Long*

Hodges, by *Ratcliffe*

Hooke by *Rogers*

Horner, by *Symes*

Hampton, by *Raymond,* Escutcheon of Pretence

Hulbert, by *Bourchier*

J.

Izod, by *Parsons*

Izod, by *Kirkham*

Jenner, and *Horton,* by *Vaulx*

Jefferies quartering *Cann,* by *Lippencott,* Escutcheon of Pretence

K.

Keck, and *Cullen,* by *Dutton*

Kyrle, by *Pury*

Kyte, by *Jayne*

L.

Lloyde, by *Hinson*

Long, by *Sampson*

Lovet, by *Pleydell*

Lunn, by *Thornton*

Lyttelton, by *Tracy*

Lygon, by *Pindar*

Lethieullier, by *Dodwell*

M.

Master, by *Oldisworth,* and by *Long*

Melbourn, by *Whittington*

Maynard, by *Colchester,* Escutcheon of Pretence

Mewx, by *Compton*

Morris, by *Bathurst*

N.

Newton, by *Stringer*

Nott, by *Rich*

Norton, by *Seaman*

O.

Or a fesse between three gryphons heads erased sable, by *Phelps*

P.

Packer, by *Surman*

Parry, by *Raynesford*

Pauncefoot, by *Rogers*

Pates by *Ockwold*

Partridge by *Fowler*

Paul, by *Peach*

Pearse, by *Peach*

Perrot, by *Payne*

Perry, by *Monoux*

Pocock, by *Caple*

Pool, by *Tracy*

Powle, by *Ireton,* Escutcheon of Pretence

Purnell, by *Wallington*

Pennyston, by *Hale*

R.

Raynesford, by *Marrowe*

Rich, by *Howe*

Riley, by *Keyt*

Rogers, by *Heyward*

Roberts, by *Jones*

Rous, by *Coster*

S.

Sackville, by *Warneford,* Escutcheon of Pretence

Small, by *Purnell*

Sedgewick, by *Slaughter*

Selfe, by *Wiatt*

Spencer, by *Keyt*

Speake, by *Dennis*

Stanley, by *Woodward*

Still, by *Dennis*

Sheppard, by *Clifford*

Smith, by *Hardwick,* Escutcheon of Pretence

[48]

Scrope, by *Howe*

Stanford, by *Stafford*

Stratford, by *Ingram*

Stokes, by *Purnell*

Speake, by *Dennis*

Sable a Unicorn, or. on a chief argent three pinks by *Hobbs*

T.

Taylor, by *Adams*

Tracy, by *Carter*

Thornhill, by *Fisher*

Townshend, by *Lawrence*

Trye, by *Cofyn*

V.

Vert a chevron undy between three gryphons rampant or. by *Monoux*

Vernon, by *Izod*

Vanderefch, by *Raymond*

Viney, by *Guife*

W.

Wade, by *Clutterbuck*

Warneford, by *Creffwell,* Efcutcheon of Pretence

Wafhbourne, by *Kingfton*

Willet, by *Selfe*

Webb de Hill, by *Sheppard,*

Efcutcheon of Pretence	*Watts*, by *Hickes*
Webb, by *Hyett*, Efcutcheon of Pretence	
	Y.
Webb, by *Griffyn*	*Yate*, by *Bromwich*, and
Williams, by *Carter*	*Yate*, by *Yate*.

☞ Thofe Arms, which are not diftinguifhed by places of refidence, are fuch as occur on monuments, and are particularly noticed in this catalogue as quartered or impaled by others.

1

ABENHALL
Abenhall

ABETOT
Earl of Worcester

ABINGDON
Dowdeswell

ABRAHALL
Kempley

ACTON
Acton

ALMERICK
Earl of Gloucester

Amos. Sculpsit Bristol

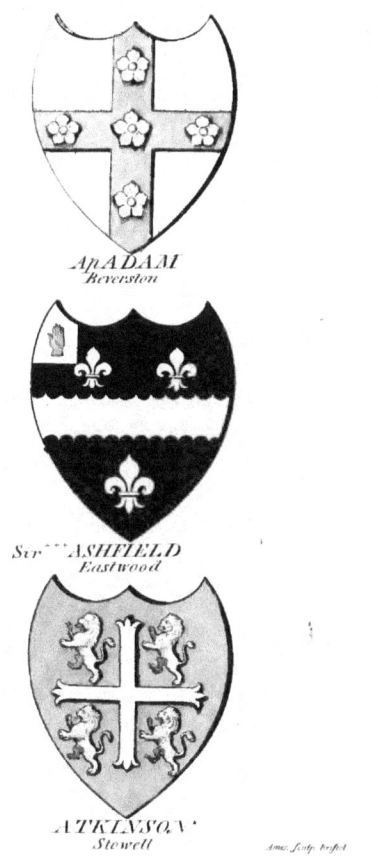
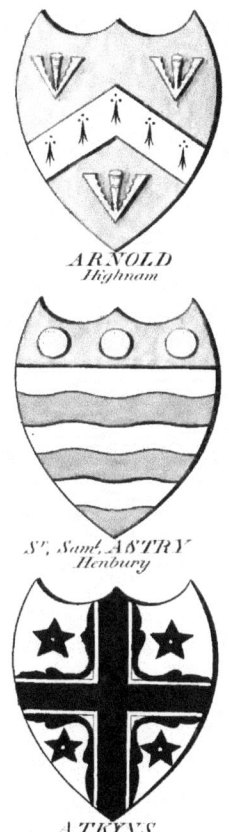

Ap ADAM
Beverston

ARNOLD
Highnam

Sir ASHFIELD
Eastwood

St. Saml. ASTRY
Henbury

ATKINSON
Stowell

ATKYNS
Saperton

AUDELEY
Earl of Gloucester

AYLEWORTH
Ayleworth

BAGHOT
Prestbury

BALL
Stonehouse

BANISTER
Turkdean

BAR
Bitton

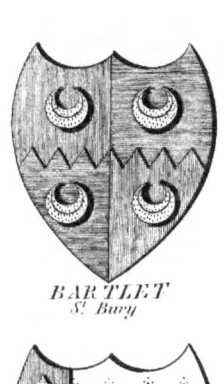
BARTLET
St Bury

BARKER
Fairford

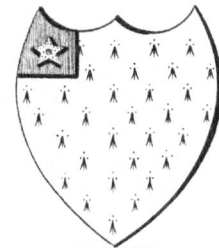
BASSET
Uly

Lord BATHURST
Cirencester

BATSON
Bourton

BAUGH
Twining

BRENT
Quenton

BREOSE
Tetbury

BRETT
Cowley

BRETT
Dodeswell

BRIDGMAN
Nimpsfield

BRIDGMAN
Prinknash

9

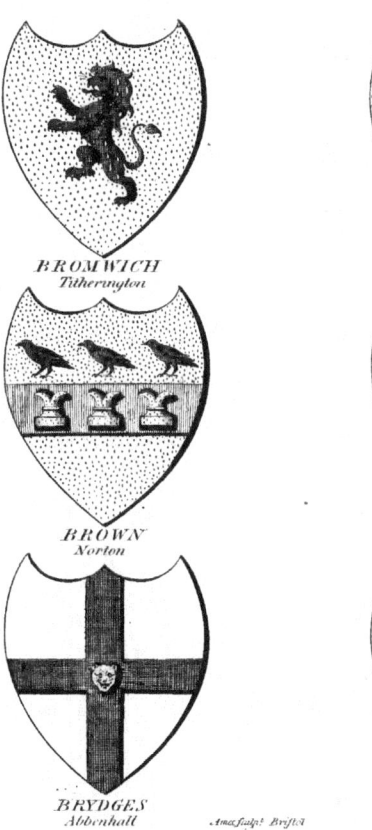

BROMWICH
Titherington

Lord BROOK

BROWN
Norton

BROWNING
Cowley

BRYDGES
Abbenhall

Amax sculp.t Brist.l

BRYDGES
Tewkesbury

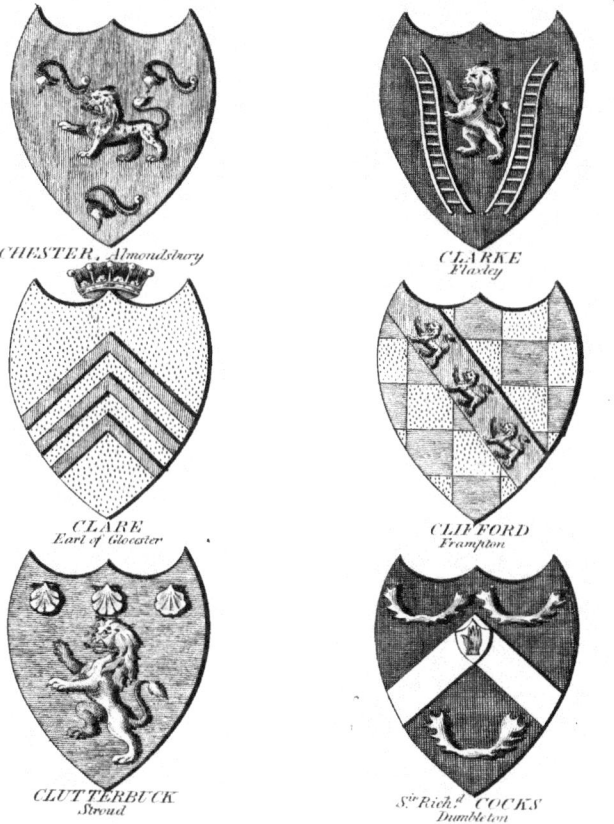

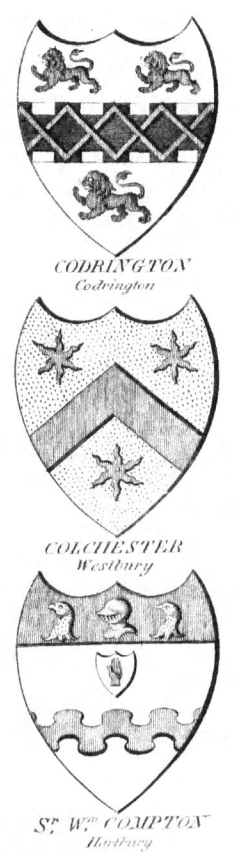

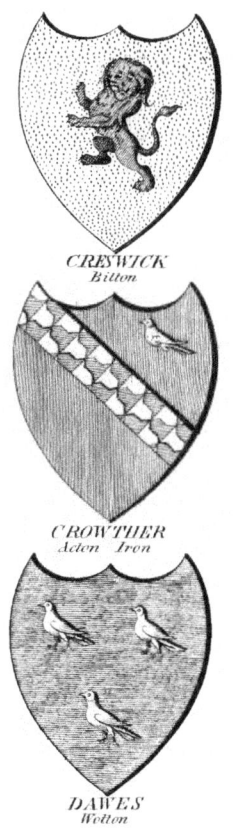

CRESWICK
Bitton

CREW
Westonbirt

CROWTHER
Acton Iron

COXWELL
Turkdean

DAWES
Wotton

Sir Thos. DAY
Easton

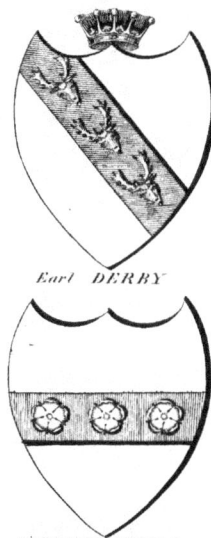

Earl DERBY

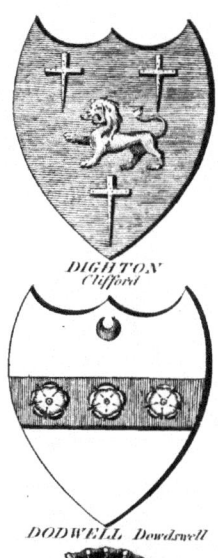

DIGHTON
Clifford

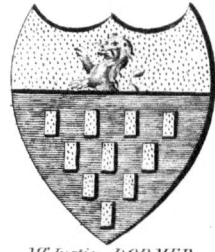

Sr Wm DODESWELL
Sevenhampton

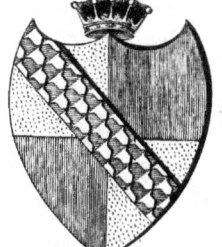

DODWELL Dowdswell

Mr Justice DORMER
Arle Court

Earl of DORSET

18

DRIVER
Avening

DUNCH
Down Amney

Sr Ralph DUTTON
Sherborn

DOWELL
Almondsbury

DUNNING
Lidney

DAUNT
Oldpen

Azer, sculp.t Bristol

ESCOURT
Shipton

FARMER
Childs Wickham

FETTYPLACE
Coln Alwins

FIELD
Stroud

FINCH
Kempley

FANE
Westbury

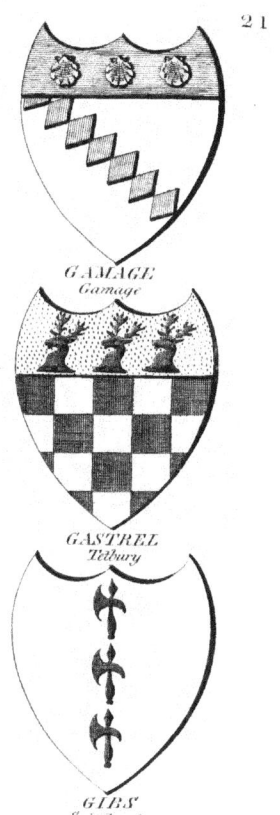

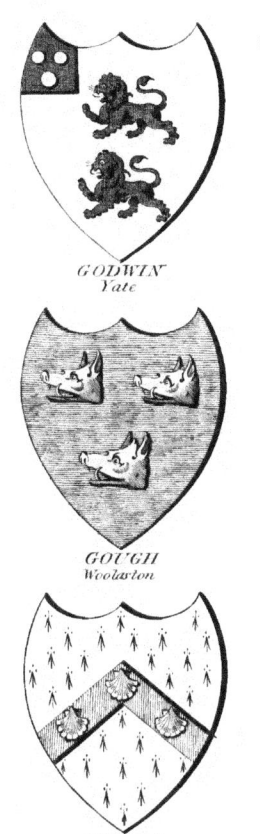

23

Lord GUILFORD

GROSSE
Sodbury

HAILES
Abbey

Sir John GUISE
Rendcomb

HALE
Alderley

Sir John HALES
Batsford

24

HALL
High Meadow

HANDELOE
Williamstrip

HARCOURT
Henbury

HANCOCKS
Twining

Sir George HANGER
Driffield

HARDWICK
Awre

25

HARRINGTON
Marshfield

HART
Bitton

HATHEWAY
Hatheway

HAYNES
Wyke & Abston

Sir Wm HICKS
Beverston

HIGFORD
Twining

26

HILL
Alveston

HOBS
Quedgley

HODGES
Clifton

HOBBY
Hailes

HODGES
Broadwell

HODGES
Shipton

27

S.r Rich.d HOLFORD Westonbirt
HOLLAND Siston
HOLME Stapleton
HOPTON Littleton
HORTON Wotton
S.r Rich.d HOWE Compton

28

HINSON
Badgworth

S.r James HOWE
Guiting

HOWE
Stowell

HUNGERFORD
Windrush

HUNTLEY
Boxwell

HUSSEY
Saperton

29

IRETON
Coln Alwins

JACKSON
Westbury

JAMES
Tidenham

JEFFERIES
Stanley

S.ir Rob.t JENKINSON
Hawksbury

S.ir Fra.s JERNINGHAM
Painswick

30

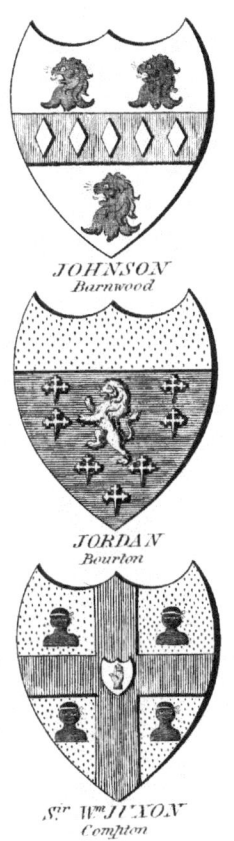

JOHNSON
Barnwood

JORDAN
Bourton

Sir Wm JUXON
Compton

JONES
Winterborn

JOYCE
Clowerwall

KEEBLE
EastLeach

32

LACIE
Guiting

LANGTON
Acton

LAWFORD
Stapleton

LAWRENCE
Badgworth

LEIGH
Addlestrop

LIGGON
Arle Court

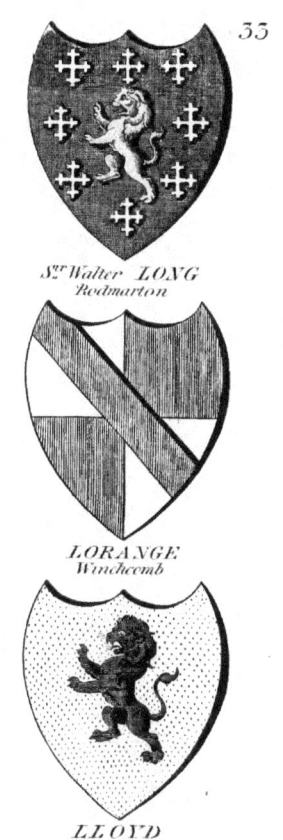

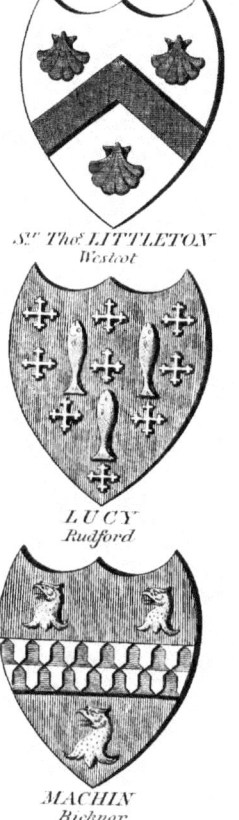
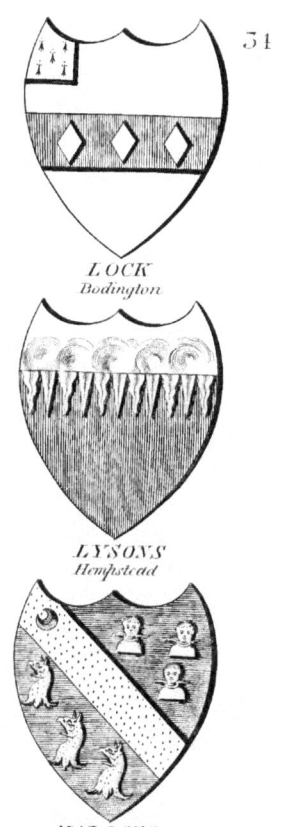

51

Sr. Thos LITTLETON
Westcot

LOCK
Bodington

LUCY
Rudford

LYSONS
Hempstead

MACHIN
Bicknor

MADOCKS
Tidenham

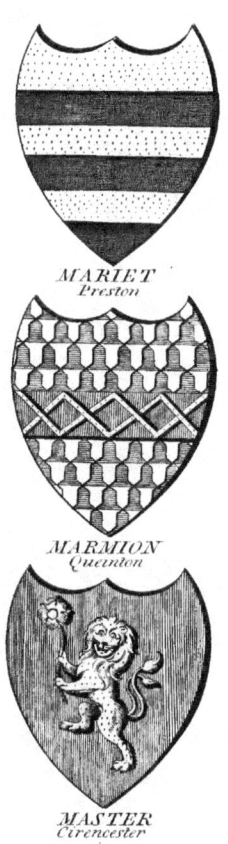
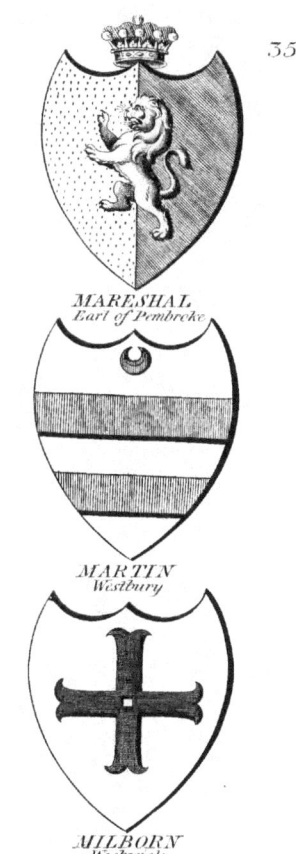

MARIET
Preston

MARESHAL
Earl of Pembroke

MARMION
Quenton

MARTIN
Westbury

MASTER
Cirencester

MILBORN
Wickwick

37

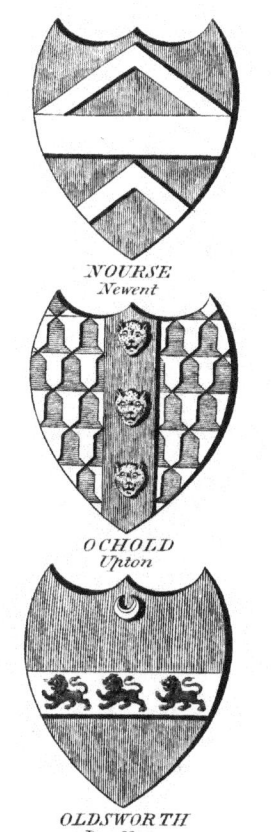

NORWOOD
Leckhampton

NOURSE
Newent

NARWENT
Newnham

OCHOLD
Upton

OLDISH
Naunton

OLDSWORTH
Bradley

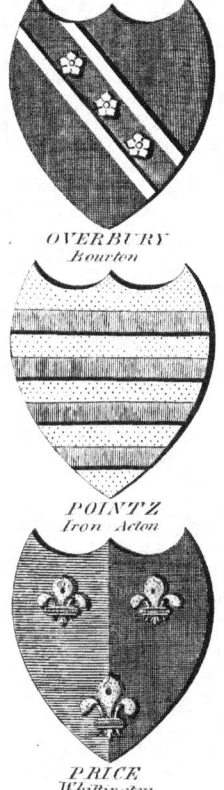

38

OVERBURY
Bourton

OWEN
Westcot

POINTZ
Iron Acton

Mr. Justice POWELL
Deerhurst

PRICE
Whittington

PURY
Taunton

PINDER
Kempty

PAIN
Painswick

PARKER
Harsfield

PYRKE
Little Dean

PARMITER
Olveston

PARSONS
Kemerton

40

PARTRIDGE
Miserden

PASTON
Horton

PAUNCEFOOT Newent

PURY
Tainton

Lord PETRE

PITT
Sudeley

41

PLAYER
Mangotsfield

POOL
Saperton

RIDLER
Edgeworth

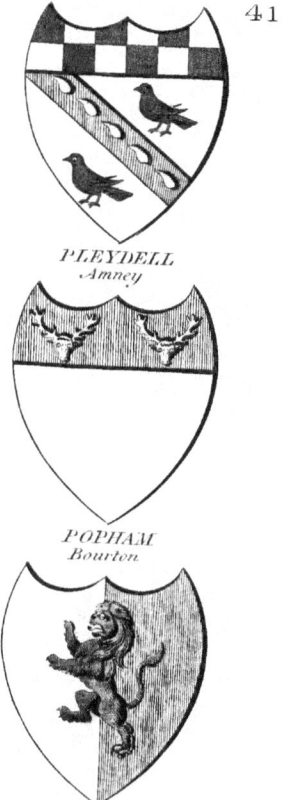

PLEYDELL
Amney

POPHAM
Bourton

ROBERTS
Haresfield

43

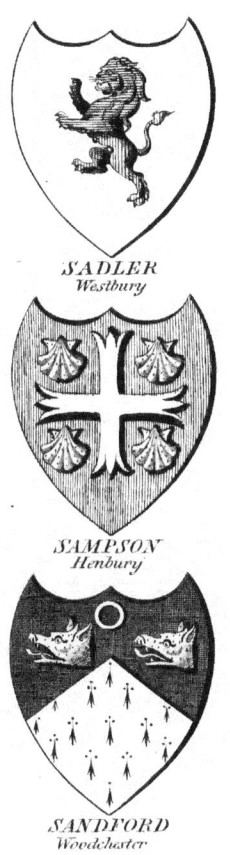

SADLER
Westbury

SAMBACH
Snowshill

SAMPSON
Henbury

St AMAND
South Cerney

SANDFORD
Woodchester

SANDYS
Miserden

44

SAVAGE
Tetbury

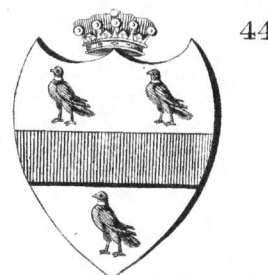
Earl of SCARBOROUGH

Lord Viscount SCUDAMORE

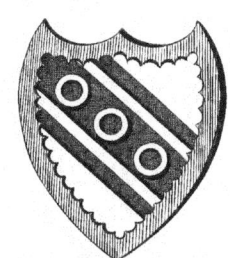
SELWYN
Matson

SEYMOUR
Bitton

SHELDON
Marston

SHEPPARD
Avening

SLAUGHTER
Slaughter

SLOPER
Iron Acton

SMITH
Campden

SMITH
Nibley

SOLERS
Shipton Solers

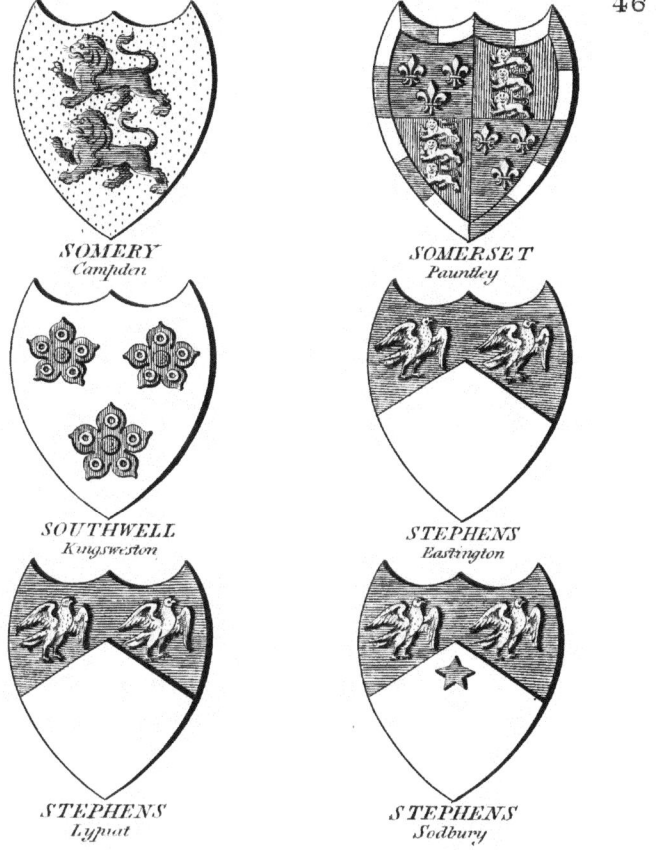

47

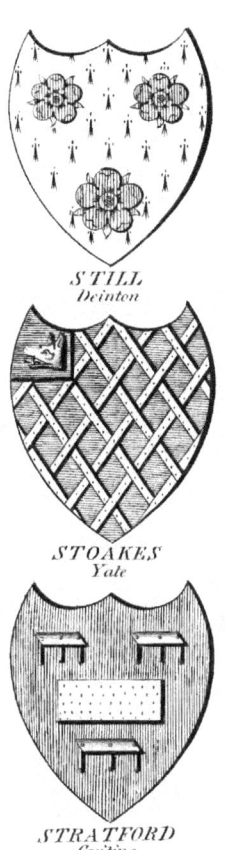
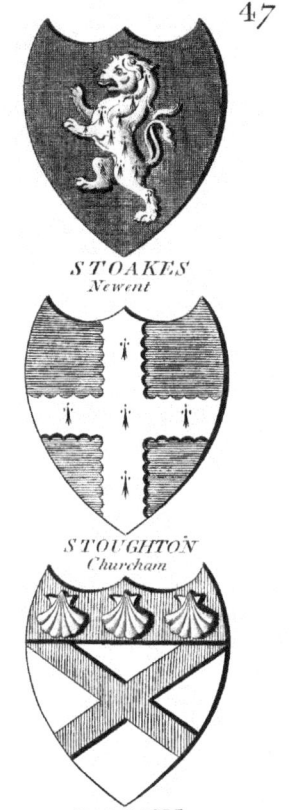

STILL
Deinton

STOAKES
Newent

STOAKES
Yate

STOUGHTON
Churcham

STRATFORD
Guiting

TALBOYS
Tetbury

48

THYNNE
Buckland

TIPPING Hawksbury

Lord Viscount TRACY
Toddington

THROGMORTON
Clower Wall

S.r John TOPP
Tormarton

TRACY
Stanway

49

TROTMAN *Siston*

VALENCE
Earl of Pembroke

VEAL
Simons Hall

TRYE
Hardwick

VAUGHAN
Ruerdean

VERE
Earl of Oxford

50

Lord VERNEY

VINEY
Tainton

Lord Viscount WEYMOUTH

WADE
Blaisden

WAKEMAN
Beckford

WALTER
Stapleton

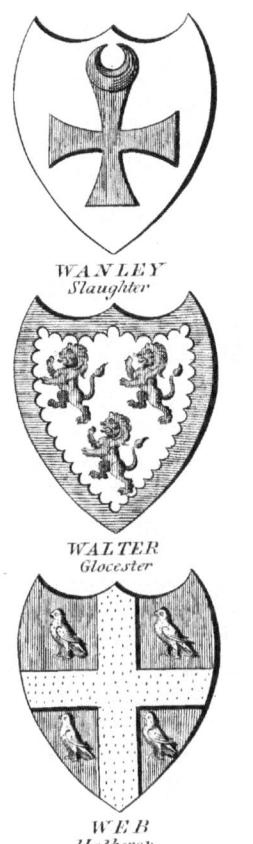

WANLEY
Slaughter

WARNFORD
Sudgrove

WALTER
Glocester

WARNER
Rodborough

WEB
Hatherop

WEB
Marshfield

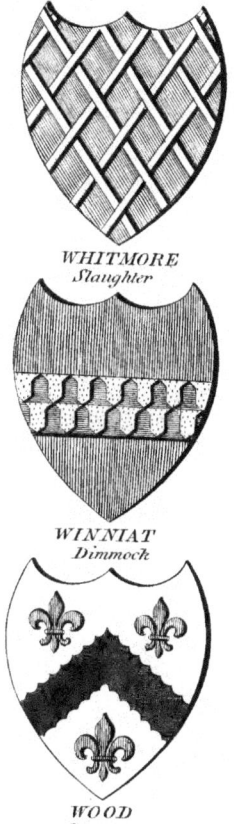

WHITTINGTON
Cold Aston

WHITMORE
Slaughter

WINDHAM
Clowerwall

WINNIAT
Dimmock

WINTOUR
Lidney

WOOD
Brockrup

53

WOODWARD
Bitton

WOODWARD
Newent

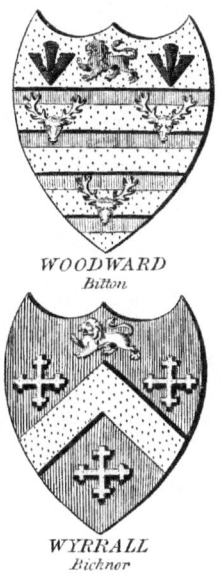

WYRRALL
Bicknor

YATE
Arlingham

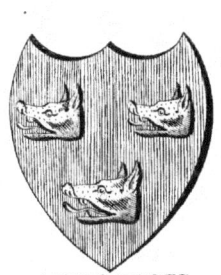

ABERCHERDER.

ADAMS
Pauntley

ADEY
Wottonunderedge

ADY
Dursley

ADYE
Cirencester

AINGE
Lechlade

55

ALDRIDGE
Stroud

ARUNDELL
Stroud

S.ʳ Rob.ᵗ AUSTEN
Churchdown

APSLEY

ATWELLS
Thornbury

AYLMER
Lord Aylmer

BABER Gloucester   BAILLIE

BAINTON Sherbourn   BAKER Almondsbury

BAKER Bybury   BALDWIN Twining

57

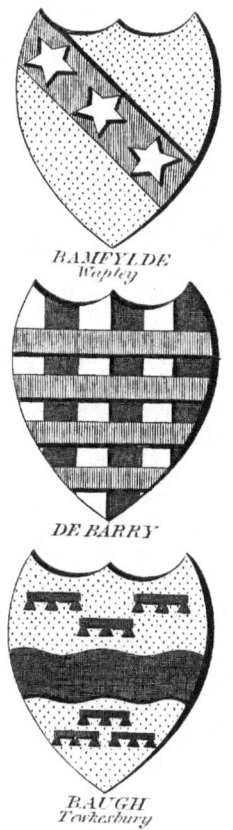

BAMFYLDE
Wapley

BAMPTON
Leachlade

DE BARRY

BATES

BAUGH
Tewkesbury

BAYLIS
New Mills

BEALE
Newent

BEARPACKER
Marshfield & Wottonunderedge

BEDFORD
Old Sodbury

BEDINGFIELD
Cleeve

BERKELEY
Rendcombe & Stoke Gifford

BELL
Glocester

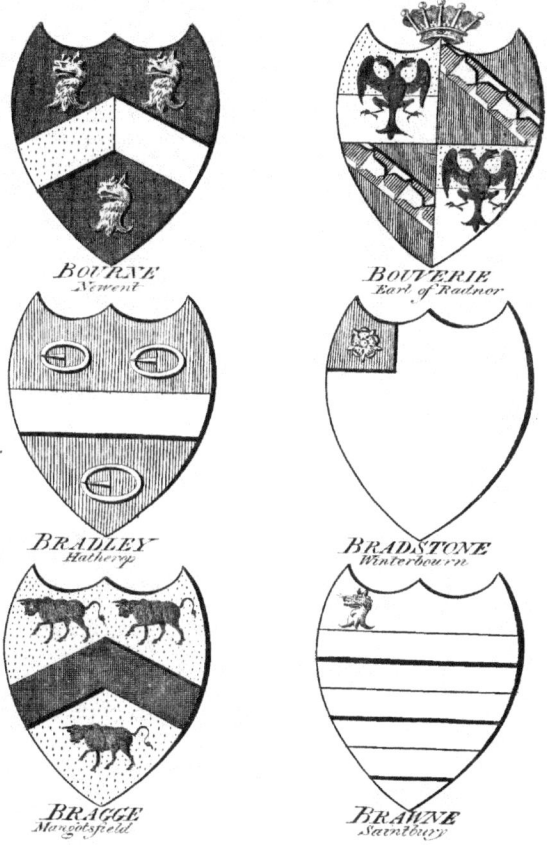

60

BOURNE
Newent

BOUVERIE
Earl of Radnor

BRADLEY
Hatherop

BRADSTONE
Winterbourn

BRAGGE
Mangotsfield

BRAWNE
Saintbury

61

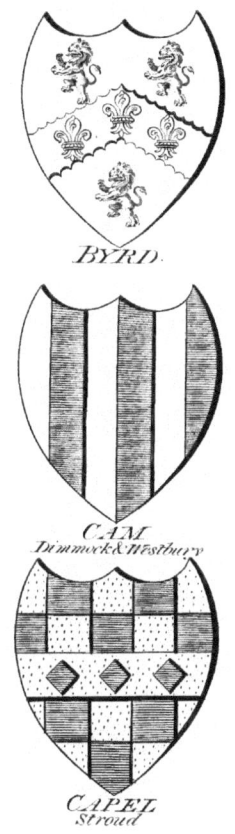

BYRD.

CALVERT
Lord Baltimore

CAM
Dimmock & Westbury

CAMBRIDGE
Wheatenhurst

CAPEL
Stroud

CAPLE
Presbury

CARDONNEL
Risington

CARPENTER
Maismore

CARTER
Cold Aston & Sevenhampton

CARTERET
Coats

CARTWRIGHT

CASSEY
Deerhurst

(3)

LIST OF SUBSCRIBERS.

A.

RIGHT Hon. Lord Apsley, *Cirencester.*
A. Austin, Esq. *Wotton-Underedge.*
Matthew Adeane, Esq. *Alderley.*
Charles Adey, Esq. *Wotton-Underedge.*
Daniel Adey, Esq. *Bath.*
Richard Aldridge, Esq. *Bristol.*
William Austin, M. D. *Oxford.*
Mr. Allaway, *Nap.*
Mr. Adey, *Dursley.*
Mr. Aycrigg, *Newent.*
Mr. Adamson, *Stroud.*

Rev. William Baker, *Dowdeswell.*
Mr. Burroughs, *Stroud.*
Mr. Baylis, *Painswick.*
Mr. Bowdler, *Tetbury.*
Mrs. Butt, *Ditto.*
Mr. Matthew Paul Bamford, *Ditto.*
Mr. John Bower, *Newent.*
Mr. H. Bower, *Ditto.*
Mr. Best, *Greenwich.*
Mr. Ballinger, *Chalford.*
Richard Bigland, Esq. *Frocester.*
Thomas Bathurst, Esq. *Lydney-Park.*

B.

His Grace the Duke of Beaufort, 2 sets, *Badminton.*
Right Hon. the Earl of Berkeley, *Berkeley-Castle.*
Hon. George Cranfield Berkeley, M. P. *London.*
T. Baghott Delabere, Esq. *Southam.*
Thomas Baylis, Esq. *Stroud.*
Henry Burgh, Esq. *Inner-Temple.*
Archer Blackwell, Esq. *Chalford.*
Edward Bayley, Esq. *Wotton-Underedge.*
Edward Bearpacker, Esq. *Ditto.*
Jeremiah Baker, Esq. *Redland-Court.*
Francis Boughton, Esq. *Avening.*
John Beale, Esq. *Newent.*
William Buckle, Esq. *Mythe.*
Charles Bragge, Esq. *Cleeve-Hill.*
Richard Bayley, Esq. *Hambrook.*
Rev. Richard Brereton, *Wotton,* near *Glocester.*
Rev. J. Biddle, *Beckford.*

C.

Sir William Codrington, Bart. *Doddington.*
Sir Thomas Crawley Bovey, Bart. *Flaxley.*
Dr. Chapman, President of Trinity College, Vice-Chancellor, *Oxford.*
Robert Campbell, Esq. *Creed-Place.*
William Capel, Esq. *Stroud.*
Henry Cook, Esq. *Ditto.*
Maynard Colchester, Esq. *Hill, Forest of Dean.*
William Cole, Esq. *Stonehouse.*
Robert Clark, Esq. *Tetbury.*
Joseph Cripps, Esq. *Cirencester.*
Estcourt Creswell, *Bibury.*
Charles Coxe, Esq. *Lypiat.*
Thomas Coker, Esq. *Deighton.*
Rev Dr. Chester, *Glocester.*
Rev. J. Collinson, *Cirencester.*
Rev. C. Coxwell, *Ablington.*

Rev.

Rev. J. Chaunler, *Southrup.*
Rev. J. Chamberlayne, *Maugersbury.*
Mrs. Colchester, *Churchdown.*
Mrs. Clarke, *Hill Herefordshire.*
Mr. J. Colborne, *Stroud.*
Mr. Alderman Colborne, *Glocester.*
Mr. Cooper, *Woodchester.*
R. B. Cheston, M. D. F. R. S. *Glocester.*
Edward Chinn, Esq. *Mout.*
Mr. Clayfield, *Bristol.*
Mr. Croome, *Stroud.*

D.

Right Hon. Lord Ducie, *Spring-Park.*
Right Rev. Lord Bishop of Durham, *Rendcomb-Park.*
John Darke, Esq. *Breedon, Worcestershire.*
Charles D'Oyley, Esq. *Southrop.*
Drummond, M. D. *Rudgeway.*
Rev. James Dallaway, *Trinity-College, Oxford.*
Rev. Edward Davis, *Winterbourn.*
Mr. Dimock, *Stonehouse.*
Mr. Deeble, *London.*

E.

Thomas Estcourt, Esq. M. P. *Estcourt-House, near Tetbury.*
Charles Edwin, Esq. *Clearwell.*
Edward Elton, Esq. *Glocester.*
Thomas Ellis, Esq. *Bath.*
Rev. W. Ellis, *Stroud.*
Mr. Ellis, *Pagan-Hill.*

Mr. Richard Eltonhead, *Glocester.*
Mr. James Elderton, *Rodborough-House.*

F.

T. E. Freeman, Esq. *Batesford.*
John Farr, Esq. *Bristol.*
P. Farr, Esq. *Ditto.*
James Fisher, Esq. *London.*
William Fryer, Esq. *Millend.*
John Fisher Weare, Esq. *Bristol.*
Samuel Farmer, Esq. *Glocester.*
Rev. J. Foley, *Newent.*
Mr. William Fisher, *Tetbury.*

G.

Sir John Guise, Bart. *Highnam.*
Right Rev. Lord Bishop of Glocester, *Glocester.*
John Gardner, Esq. *Painswick.*
K. Grove, Esq. *Thornbury.*
Rev. P. Grande, *Dirham.*
Mr. Gyde, *Bath.*
Mr. Grazebrook, *Stroud.*

H.

J. W. Horlock, Esq. *Ashwicke.*
Samuel Hayward, Esq. *Sandhurst.*

Charles

Charles Hayward, Esq. *Quedgley.*
Doddington Hunt, Esq. *Charlton.*
John Howell, Esq. *Prinknash.*
John Hawker, Esq. *Dudbridge.*
Benjamin Hyett, Esq. *Painswick.*
John Hollings, Esq. *Stroud.*
B. Hobhouse, Esq. *Redland.*
Samuel Harford, Esq. *Bristol.*
Richard Haynes, Esq. *Wick and Abson.*
W. H. Hicks, M. D. *Glocester.*
Dr. Hardwick, *Sodbury.*
Rev. ——— Hayward, *Tewkesbury.*
Rev. ——— Hayward, *Withington.*
Rev. ——— Hayward, *Frocester.*
Rev. ——— Hippisley, *Stow.*
Rev. ——— Higford, *Dixton.*
Hallaway, Esq. *Froom-Hall.*
Mr. Hoskins, *Tetbury.*
Mr. Hicks, *Berkeley.*
Mr. Hankins *Dymock.*
Mr. Charles Higgs, *Cheltenham.*
Mr. Hope, *Glocester.*
Mr. Harden, *Cirencester.*
Mr. Hawker, *Uley.*
Mr. Hill, *Stonehouse.*
Mr. Heaven, *Hampton.*
Mr. Harward, *Glocester.*

J.

Roynon Jones, Esq. *Hayhill.*
Thomas Ingram, Esq. *Coln St. Aldwin's.*
Mr. Edwin Jeynes, *Glocester.*
Mrs. Jackson, *Sneed-Park.*
Mrs. Jones, *Stroud.*
Mr. Jenner, *Ditto.*
Rev. J. Jayne, *Rendcomb.*

K.

William Knight, Esq. *Stroud.*
R. Kingscote, Esq. *Kingscote.*
Richard King, Esq. *Alkerton.*
Mr. King, *Dursley.*
Francis Knight, Esq.

L.

Lady Lippincott, *Stoke-Bishop.*
James Henry, Leigh, Esq. *Addlestrop.*
Robert Loder, Esq. *Leachlade.*
Samuel Lewes, Esq. *Blaize-Castle.*
D. Lysons, M. D. *Bath.*
Rev. S. Lysons, *Rodmarton.*
Rev. J. Lifely, *Leachlade.*
Mrs. Leigh, *Broadwell.*
Mr. Leversage, *Lypiat.*
Mrs. Lane. *Glocester.*

M.

Thomas Master, Esq. M. P. *Cirencester.*
C. T. Morgan, Esq. *Hempstead.*
Samuel Munkley, Esq. *Bristol.*
Thomas Mee, Esq. *Glocester.*
Thomas Morse, Esq. *Dursley.*
Dr. Merewether, *Marshfield.*
Mr. Morris, *Barnwood-Court.*
Mr. Miles, *Leonard-Stanley.*
Mr. Mitchel, *Randwick.*

N.

His Grace the Duke of Norfolk, E. M.
New College Library, *Oxford.*

William

(6)

William Naper, Esq. *Slaughter.*
Rev John Newton, *Glocester.*
Rev. B. Newton, *Ditto.*
Mr. Richard Nayler, *Ditto.*
Mr. Norton, *Bristol.*
Lieut. Nayler, *Portsmouth.*

O.

Right Hon. the Earl of Orford, *Srawberry-Hill.*
Mrs. Osborn, *Monk's-Mill.*
Mr. Thomas Oatridge, *Leachlade.*
Mr. Daniel Oatridge, *Tetbury.*

P.

Sir G. O. Paul, Bart. *Rodborough.*
Edward Probyn, Esq. *Newland.*
Thomas Pettat, Esq. *Stanley.*
Thomas Purnell Purnell, Esq. *King's-Hill.*
Nathaniel Peach, Esq. *Bownham-House.*
Samuel Phillimore, Esq. *Dursley.*
William Purnell, Esq. *Dursley New-House.*
Samuel Peach, Esq. *Tockington.*
John Paul, Esq. *Tetbury.*
J. De La Field Phelps, Esq. *Dursley.*
John Parsons, Esq. *Kemerton.*
Rev. —— Price, *Bodleian Library Oxford.*
Rev. John Pettat, *Stonehouse.*
Mr. Partridge, *Bowbridge.*
Mr. Obadiah, Paul, *Rodborough.*
Mr. Pulton, *Painswick.*
Mr William Pitt, *Glocester.*
Mr. Pain, *Stroud.*

R.

Sir John Read, Bart. *Oddington.*
William Raikes, Esq. *London.*
Thomas Raikes, Esq. *Ditto.*
C. Raikes, Esq. *Ditto.*
R. Raikes, Esq. *Glocester.*
Edward Rogers, Esq. *Dowdeswell.*
Mr. Thomas Rogers, *Ditto.*
—— Raymond, Esq. *London.*
S. Richardson, Esq. *Newent.*
Mr. Thomas Richardson, *Ditto.*
Rev. Richard Rogers, *Glocester.*
Rev. Samuel Rogers, *Ditto.*
Rev. —— Rice, *Quinington.*
Mr. John Rice, *Bourton-on-the-Water.*
Mr. John Roberts, *Chalford.*
William Read, Esq. *Ebley.*

S.

Sir John Hugh Smyth, Bart. *Long Ashton-Court.*
Rev. J. Small, D. D. *Bristol.*
Peter Snell, Esq. *Whitley-Court.*
J. Skipp, Esq. *Stonehouse.*
Abraham Saunders, Esq. *Glocester.*
Thomas Smyth, Esq. *Stapleton.*
Thomas Shurmur, Esq. *Frogmarsh.*
T. Saunders, Esq. *Tetbury.*
R. Saunders, Esq. *Little Farringdon.*
John Small, Esq. *Cirencester.*
H. B. Scudamore, Esq. *Newent.*
Edward Sampson, Esq. *Henbury.*
Robert Street, Esq. *Aust.*
Powell Snell, Esq. *Guiting.*
S. Snowden, M. D. *Rodborough.*
D. Skeet, L. L. D. *Bath.*
Rev. —— Savage, *Tetbury.*
Capt. Selwyn, 7th regiment, Royal Fuzileers, *Glocester.*
Mr. William Savill, *Chalford.*

Mr.

Mr. Thomas Shurmur, *Woodchester.*
Mr. Rowles, Scudamore, *Stroud.*
Mr. Smith, *Wallbridge.*
Mr. John Smith, *Painfwick.*
Thomas Shellard, Esq. *Redland.*
Samuel Span, Esq. *Briſtol.*

T.

Right Hon. Lord Viſcount Tracey, *Toddington.*
Theyer Townſend, Esq. *Steanbridge.*
John Tyler, Esq. *Redland.*
Thomas Tyndale, Esq. *Briſtol.*
Thomas Tyndale, Jun. Esq. *Ditto.*
Trinity College Library, *Oxford.*
Rev. W. D. Tatterfall, *Wotton-Underedge.*
Mrs. Tracey, *Sandywell-Park.*
Mr. C. B. Trye, *Gloceſter.*
Mr. William Tayloe, *Chalford.*
Mr. Tanner, *Stroud.*
Mr. John Trotman, *Chalford.*
Mr. J. P. Tippetts, *Tetbury.*
Mr. John Trotman, *Winchcomb.*
Mr. Thornton, *Stroud.*
Mr. J. Turner, *Gloceſter.*

V.

Goodſon Vines, Esq. *Wotton-Underedge.*
Rev. Edward Vernon, *Bourton-on-the-Water.*

W.

Sir Thomas Wheate, Bart. *Leachlade.*
John Webb, Esq. M. P. *Cote* near *Briſtol.*
A. T. Withers, Esq.
N. Winchcomb, Esq. *Stroud.*
John Wade, Esq. *Pudhill.*
Edward Wilbraham, Esq. *Horſley.*
William Wakeman, Esq. *Beckford.*
Samuel Webb, Esq. *Painfwick.*
Charles Williams, Esq. *Tidenham.*
Thomas Whittington, Esq. *Hamfwell.*
Thomas White, Esq. *Stroud.*
Rev. T. Croome Wickes, D. D. *Tetbury.*
Rev. James Webſter, D. D. *Durſley.*
Rev. Profeſſor White, *Oxford.*
Mr. Joſeph Wathen, *Stroud.*
Mr. C. H. Wilton, *London.*
Samuel Windowe, Esq. *Stroud.*
Mr. Henry Windowe, *Ryeford.*
Thomas Wathen, Esq. *Stanley.*
Mrs. Wickes, *Tetbury.*
Miſs E. Wick, *Wick-ſtreet.*
Mr. Wm. Wood, Jun. *Tetbury.*
Mr. John Wallington, *Durſley.*
Mr. William Wells, *Leachlade.*
Mr. William Ward, *Stroud.*
Mr. Henry Wilton, Jun. *Gloceſter.*
Mr. C. White, *Dudbridge.*
Mr. R. Webb, *Stroud.*

Y.

Rev. H. G. D. Yate, *Broomſterror.*

Milton Keynes UK
Ingram Content Group UK Ltd.
UKHW040042180324
439604UK00006B/924